SHOUT OUT BOO 2

To Billy + Noel
Have lots of fun
Shouting out
BOO!!

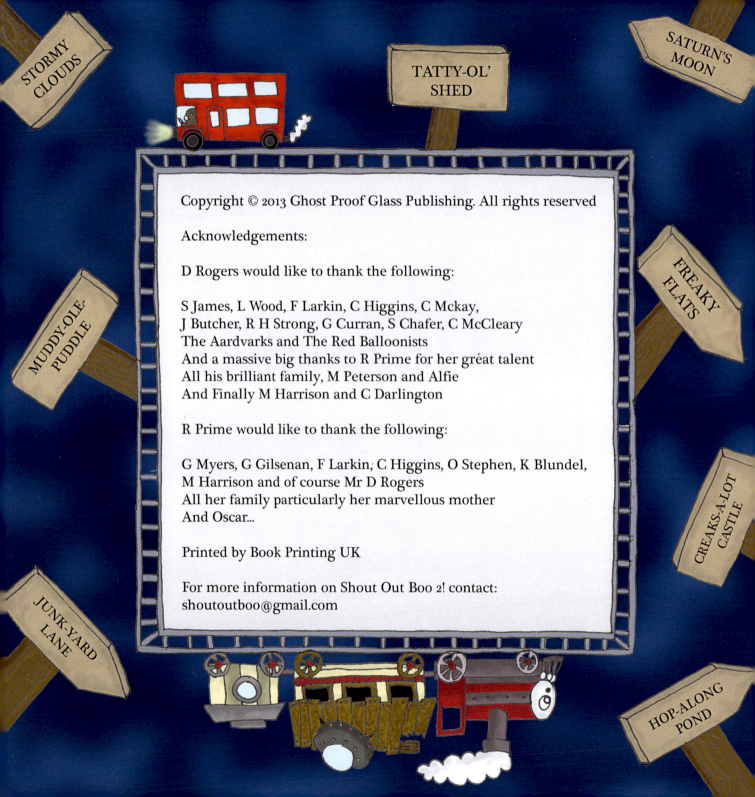

Copyright © 2013 Ghost Proof Glass Publishing. All rights reserved

Acknowledgements:

D Rogers would like to thank the following:

S James, L Wood, F Larkin, C Higgins, C Mckay,
J Butcher, R H Strong, G Curran, S Chafer, C McCleary
The Aardvarks and The Red Balloonists
And a massive big thanks to R Prime for her great talent
All his brilliant family, M Peterson and Alfie
And Finally M Harrison and C Darlington

R Prime would like to thank the following:

G Myers, G Gilsenan, F Larkin, C Higgins, O Stephen, K Blundel,
M Harrison and of course Mr D Rogers
All her family particularly her marvellous mother
And Oscar...

Printed by Book Printing UK

For more information on Shout Out Boo 2! contact:
shoutoutboo@gmail.com

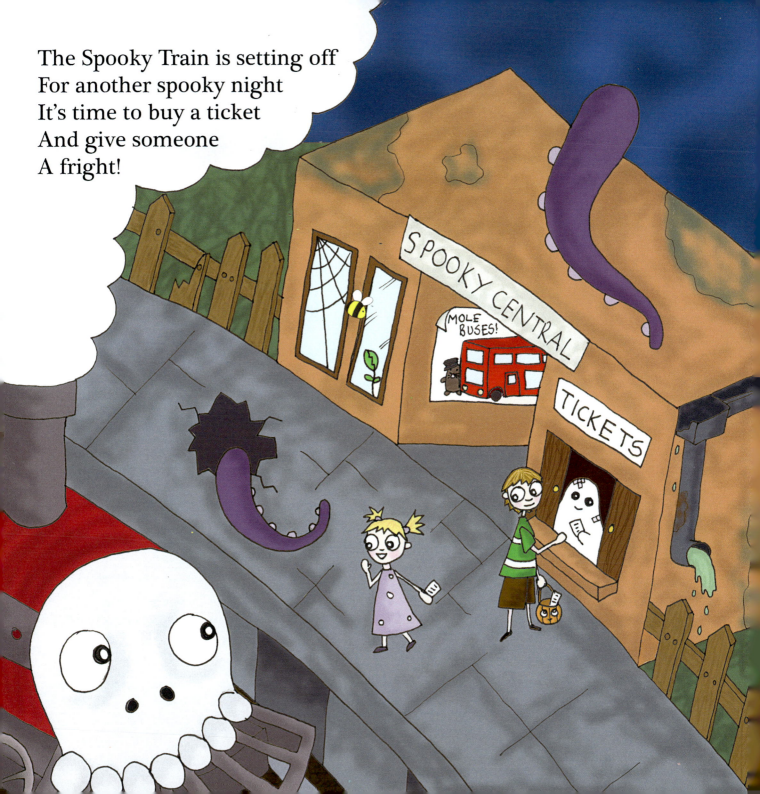

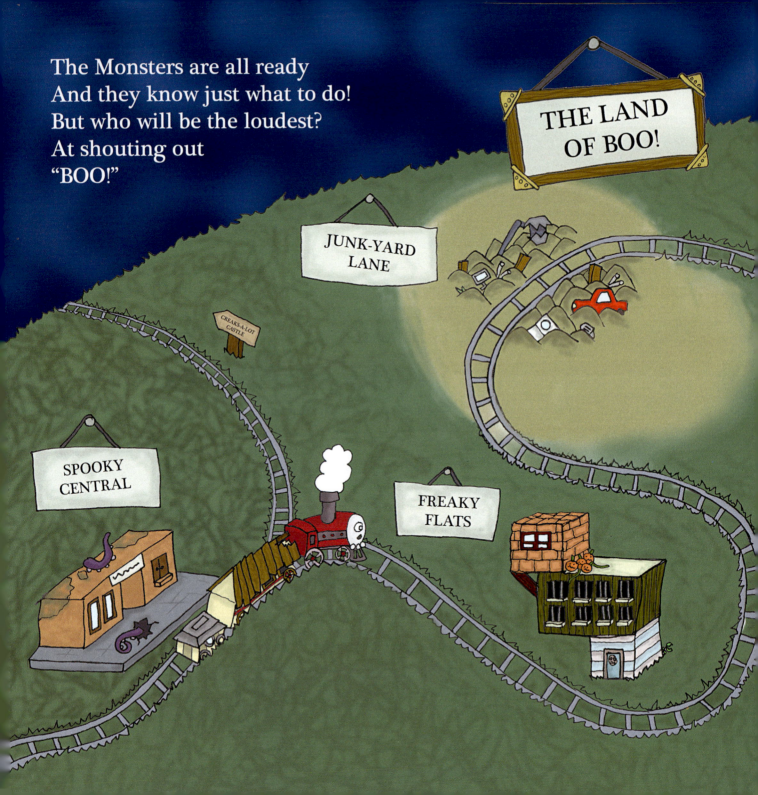

SATURN'S MOON

TATTY-OL' SHED

GRAND SPOOKY CENTRAL

Let's blow the whistle "PEEP PEEP!"
And start the train "CHUFF CHUFF!"
It's time to leave the station!
But who will be waiting down the line
At our next destination?

It's Wendy the Werewolf!
Who is covered in fur
And lives in Freaky Flats!
She loves howling at the moon
And chasing Clever Cats!

Then when she's finished chasing
She knows just what to do...
She wiggles her nose and wags her tail...
And shouts out...

Do you think she is best?
And will give the BIGGEST scare?
Or shall we go to the next station
And see who's waiting there?

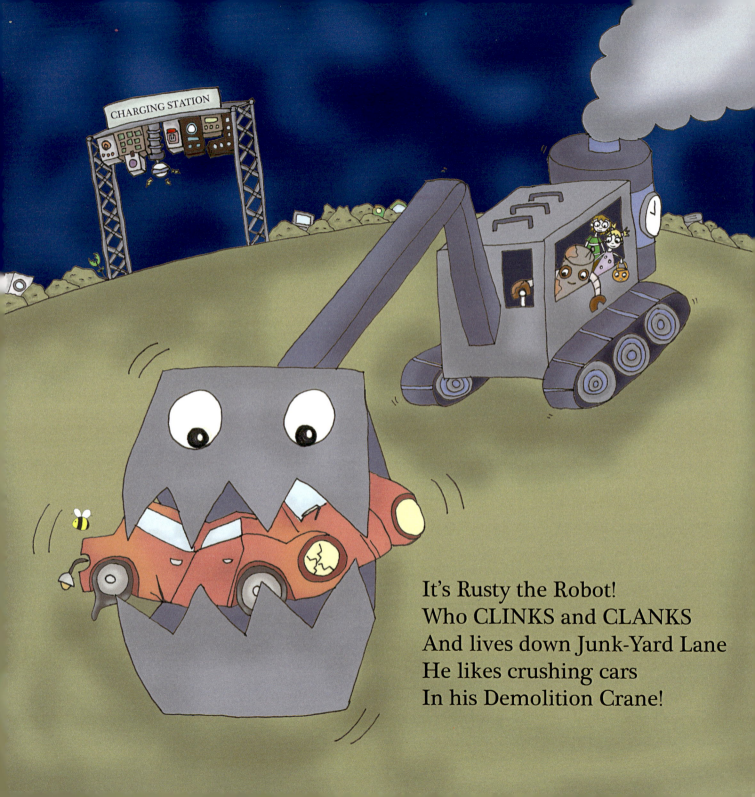

It's Rusty the Robot!
Who CLINKS and CLANKS
And lives down Junk-Yard Lane
He likes crushing cars
In his Demolition Crane!

Then when he's finished crushing
He knows just what to do...
He charges up his batteries...
And shouts out...

Do you think he is best?
And will give the BIGGEST scare?
Or shall we go to the next station
And see who's waiting there?

Do you think he is best
And will give the BIGGEST scare?
Or shall we go to the next station
And see who's waiting there?

It's Minsey the Martian!
Who zooms through space
And lives on Saturn's Moon.
She loves blasting asteroids
And making things go BOOM!

Then when she's finished blasting
She knows just what to do...
She whizzes past, VERY fast...
And shouts out...

Do you think she is best?
And will give the BIGGEST scare?
Or shall we go to the next station
And see who's waiting there?

The Train has reached its final stop
And the Monsters are all there!
But which one do you think
Will give the BIGGEST scare?

If you're not sure don't worry!
Because you know just what to do...
Just turn around and VERY loud...

Shout out...